rainbows

What's the Weather?

Helen Barden

Illustrated by
Katy Sleight

Evans

4

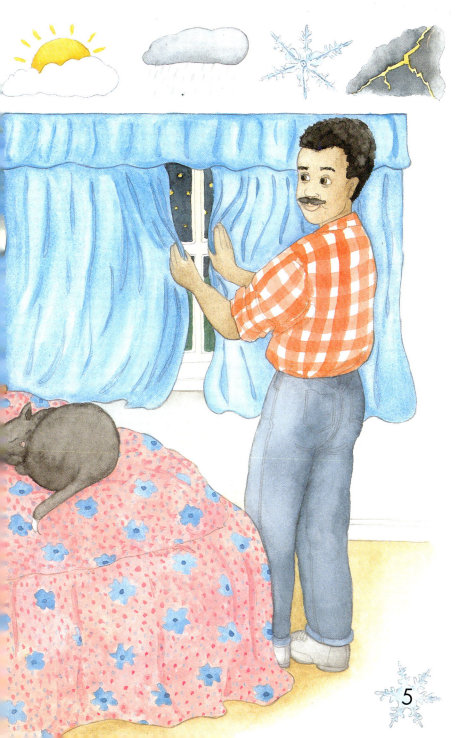

5

If it rains I can...

splash in the puddles,

or put up my umbrella.

Do you know that birds wash their feathers in the rain?

If it is windy I can...

play with my kite,

or blow bubbles.

In autumn, the wind blows the leaves off the trees.

If it is frosty I can...

break off the icicles,

or slide on the ice.

10

Frost makes the spider's web sparkle.

If it snows I can...

build a snowman,

or play on my sledge.

12

You can see animal
tracks in the snow.

If it is stormy I can...

watch the lightning,

and listen to the thunder.

Sheep huddle together in a storm.

If it's sunny I can...

play in my paddling pool,

and wear my shorts and T-shirt.

Butterflies visit the flowers in the sunshine.

I hope it's sunny,
then I can...

work in the garden,

and dry the washing.

18

On sunny days you can hear
the bees buzzing.

If it's foggy I can...

play in the house,

and watch TV.

Cows and trees look
mysterious in the fog.

If there is a hurricane I can...

listen to the weather report,

and look after my pets.

Nothing likes to be out in
a hurricane.

If it's cloudy...

I won't know what to wear.

It could start to rain...

...or the sun could peep
through the clouds.

25

But it's sunny, too, and guess
what I can see?

Which of these things would you need for rainy weather, sunny weather, frosty weather, snowy weather and windy weather?